BEFORE

Push Comes to Shove

Building Conflict Resolution Skills with Children

by Nancy Carlsson-Paige and Diane E. Levin
with illustrations by Celeste Henriquez

Redleaf Press

© 1998 Nancy Carlsson-Paige and Diane E. Levin
Illustrations by Celeste Henriquez

Published by: Redleaf Press
                a division of Resources for Child Caring
                450 N. Syndicate, Suite 5
                St. Paul, MN 55104-4125

Distributed by: Gryphon House
                Mailing address:
                P.O. Box 207
                Beltsville, MD 20704-0207

Library of Congress Cataloging-in-Publication Data

Carlsson-Paige, Nancy.
     Before push comes to shove : building conflict resolution skills
with children / by Nancy Carlsson-Paige and Diane E. Levin ; with
illustrations by Celeste Henriquez.
         p.   cm.
     Includes bibliographical references.
     ISBN 1-884834-53-1
     1. Conflict management—Study and teaching (Primary)—United
States. 2. School violence—United States—Prevention.
  3. Classroom management—United States. 4. Carlsson-Paige, Nancy.
Best day of the week.   I. Levin, Diane E.   II. Title.
     LB3013.3.C38   1998
     371.4'04—dc21   98-14644
                                                  CIP

This book is dedicated to teachers of young children

with deep appreciation for all that you do.

Acknowledgments

We wish to thank Zell Draz who, through her many years of teaching conflict resolution in prisons, has come to deeply appreciate the importance of teaching conflict resolution skills to children beginning at an early age. Thank you Zell, for being the steady support behind so much of our work. Sincere thanks to William Kreidler for first showing us how conflict resolution can become a subject of great interest and importance to young children and for sharing his ideas and his work so willingly with us. Special thanks to Jim Alpsburg, Jonathan Belber, Meg Bruton, Betsy Damien, Christine Gerzon, Jolinda McClellan, and Melissa Tonachel and the children in their classrooms, all of whom contributed to our understanding of the ideas presented in this book. We also wish to thank Beverly Jean Smith for helping with the wording used in Best Day of the Week. Finally, we wish to thank both Lesley College and Wheelock College for the many ways they have supported our work for many years.

Table of Contents

PART 1

Before You Begin

CHAPTER 1

Why Teach Conflict Resolution to Young Children?

A school principal said to us recently, "By fourth grade it's already too late for children to learn how to get along. They've learned to be violent by then. We didn't see this years ago, but now children fight a lot, get hurt on the playground, and kick and hit each other in the halls. We need to start teaching conflict resolution skills to kids at a much younger age."

This principal recognizes the growing problem of violence and aggression among children in the everyday life of the school. Children are living in a "socially toxic environment" that undermines their healthy social development[1]. Over and over again—in their own life experiences, on TV news, and in children's entertainment, media, and toys—children see that "might makes right," that winning is the most important thing, and that hurting others with words and actions is a regular, normal part of daily life. Not only does this climate make it difficult for children to develop tools for solving their conflicts in nonviolent and creative ways, it also makes it harder for teachers to create classroom environments that foster the moral and social development of all children.

Few teachers are prepared to deal with the problems created by children's exposure to so much disrespectful behavior and violence; few of them learned conflict resolution as part of their teacher education program. Many teachers know how to create a curriculum that helps young children con-

---

1. This concept comes from James Garbarino, *Raising Children in a Socially Toxic Environment* (San Francisco: Jossey-Bass, 1995).

struct ideas in the areas of literacy and math. It is harder to get beyond traditional curricular areas and what is commonly called "discipline" or "behavior management" to help children build knowledge and skills in the social and moral domain. Yet, increasingly in these times, children need curriculum that provides active, first-hand experiences that foster social and moral understanding and provides opportunities to learn tools for resolving conflicts peacefully.

This curriculum guide will help you begin to teach conflict resolution skills to young children, equipping them with social skills to counteract the effects of the violent world in which they live. It takes you through a process you can use to teach these skills to children, using the children's book *Best Day of the Week* as a place to start. *Best Day of the Week* can serve as a springboard for teaching the many conflict resolution skills and concepts described here, which you then can continue to work on using other books and classroom activities.

A book offers a powerful way to teach young children about conflict resolution. It provides meaningful situations that children can connect to their own experiences. This is how young children best learn conflict resolution skills—by relating the skills to their own lives and trying them out, with your help, in meaningful situations.

Building conflict resolution skills in a meaningful context also means that children need opportunities to practice and develop these skills in their daily classroom life. Once you have started using *Best Day of the Week* to teach conflict resolution, we will describe many possible ways you can build conflict resolution skills in your entire classroom curriculum.

For many teachers, working with children's conflicts in the ways described in this guide will be new. Many of us have not had positive experiences with conflict in our own lives and have not had the opportunity to learn the conflict resolution skills described here. Hopefully this story and guide will help you do new kinds of conflict resolution work with children and will encourage you to learn more about how these skills can enrich your own life too.

The good news about a conflict resolution curriculum is that it can provide children with a special power that opens new doors for interacting positively with their world. In many situations we have seen the genuine excitement, creativity, and joy that is unleashed in children who learn to use these skills. They discover a satisfaction and sense of empowerment when they can create positive social relationships and solve their problems with others. Their exuberance stands in stark contrast to the fleeting, pseudo-power children often feel when they express antisocial behaviors or violence toward others.

How Young Children Make Sense of Conflict Resolution

It takes a long time to learn the many skills and concepts involved in positive conflict resolution, and we can begin teaching them to children at a very young age. Children build their own understanding of conflict gradually, out of their experiences. Their ideas are shaped by developmental factors and by the sociocultural context in which they live. Children's ideas about conflict are different from those of adults, and each child's ideas about conflict are unique to that child. The more we are aware of how young children make sense of their world, the more effective our efforts will be.

Developmental Factors

The characteristics of young children's thinking affect how they think about and understand conflict. Keeping these characteristics in mind can help you shape your efforts to teach conflict resolution to the capabilities, interests, and needs of the children:

Children's understanding of conflict progresses from concrete to more abstract. What stands out to younger children are the visible features and actions that are part of conflict, rather than less tangible aspects of conflict, like people's internal motivations and intentions. For example, a younger child knows that people are angry because they have angry expressions on their faces, whereas an older child more easily understands that people might be angry even if they don't look angry.

Children's thinking moves gradually from static to more dynamic. At first, young children tend to think about only one aspect of a conflict at a time, but gradually they are able to think about several aspects of a conflict at once and to relate these different ideas. For example, a younger child might think that the only way out of a conflict is to get the toy she wants. In contrast, an older child is better able to imagine different solutions, such as taking turns, sharing the toy, or getting something else to play with.

Children gradually learn how to make logical causal connections in conflict. Over time, young children come to understand how their actions affect others and how other people's actions affect them. Slowly, they can get better at predicting how certain actions might bring certain reactions in conflict situations. So while a younger child might need help understanding what will happen if she grabs a toy away from someone else, an older child can imagine what someone else will do or feel as a result of what she does.

Sociocultural Context

A kindergarten class is outside for free play when Devin, Lee, and Tanya have the following conflict:

> *Devin is playing in the sandbox, building a road and running work vehicles*
> *over it. Lee comes over, stands outside the sandbox, and says, "Can I play?"*
> *Devin says, "No, there's no room. I'm making a road."*
> *Lee asks, "Can I make the road too?"*
> *"No," says Devin. "I'm doing it."*
> *Tanya comes over, steps into the sandbox, and starts pushing the sand to*
> *make a mound.*
> *Devin shouts, "NO!"*
> *Tanya looks at Devin and gently makes the mound bigger. Devin clenches*
> *his fists at Tanya and yells, "I'm playing here!" As he shakes his arms at her,*
> *she quickly gets up and runs away, heading toward the swings.*
> *Lee has been watching the whole time. He says to Devin, "You have to share*
> *the sand," and then restates the class rule, "Four kids can play in sand."*

You can see that each five year old has a unique way of dealing with conflict. In this culturally diverse kindergarten, each child has brought to the conflict a rich personal history of experience with conflict, each embedded in a social context that is layered by family, community, culture, and societal influences that affect what happens here.

Devin enters the conflict on the offense, using both his words and his hands to fight. Lee remains on the periphery of the conflict and uses words as a way of trying to get along with others. Tanya seems to try to avoid the conflict until she is facing those shaking fists of Devin's, and then she flees from the situation completely.

Individual children bring their own unique conflict histories and styles to the conflicts they have in the classroom. The more diverse the children's backgrounds and experiences, the more diverse their feelings and ideas about conflict and how to manage it, even among children at a similar developmental level.

Your efforts to teach conflict resolution will be more effective if you can closely relate your work in conflict resolution to how children are making sense of conflict. Vital to doing this is developing your own awareness of the range of possible ways different children might experience and understand conflict.

Appreciating Diversity

To develop an appreciation of the diverse ways young children experience conflict:

1. Observe how different children relate to conflict, asking yourself these questions:

> What kinds of conflicts do different children have? Are the conflicts:
> - over sharing materials?
> - over whom to play with or how to play together?
> - with individual children or larger groups?
> - with particular children?
> - during particular times of the day?
>
> How do different children deal with the conflicts they have? What approach to conflict resolution seems familiar and comfortable for each child? Do they tend to:
> - fight with fists?
> - be aggressive with words?
> - use words to try to work things out with each other?
> - avoid the conflict and give in or run away?
> - cry or seem overwhelmed?
>
> What is the range of ways that children's conflicts get successfully resolved?

What are some of the ways that children's diverse family backgrounds and cultural experiences might play a role in their conflicts and how they solve them?

2. Reflect on how your own background and experiences may have affected how you deal with conflict. If possible, find a colleague to talk with about these questions:

How do I feel about and deal with my own conflicts?

What have been my experiences with conflict in the past?

How has my own cultural experience shaped my view of conflict and how I deal with it in my personal life and in my work with children?

3. Analyze how you deal with children's conflicts by asking yourself:

How do I feel about the conflicts the children have?

What role do I play in children's conflicts?

What are some of the things I am already doing in my classroom to deal with conflicts? How are they working? What are the trouble spots?

When I help children work out their conflicts, how do I take culture and development into account?

4. Find ways to connect classroom activities to children's own meanings of and experiences with conflict in the classroom. For instance, when you read a conflict story, ask children questions about the conflicts they have in their own lives.

5. Try to adapt your approach to conflict resolution to the meanings, experiences, and style of each child. For instance, in Devin, Lee, and Tanya's class, the teacher could use puppets during a class meeting to act out a conflict that happened in the sand area. The teacher could show how the three puppets approach the conflict differently. For further information on using puppets, see chapter 9.

CHAPTER 3

Concepts and Skills Underlying Conflict Resolution

Many specific concepts and skills are involved in conflict resolution, each requiring a lot of complex thinking to understand. Children go through a long process to develop this understanding. Their ideas about each of these concepts and skills change over time, gradually coming closer and closer to the understanding adults have. As we discuss each of the concepts or skills in this chapter, we will also show you how young children begin to make sense of them.

If you have not yet read Best Day of the Week, it would be good to do that now. We will be using the story to illustrate the skills and concepts involved in peaceful conflict resolution. The story is included in this text beginning on page 23. The book may be purchased separately through Redleaf Press at 1-800-423-8309 or be requested at your local bookstore.

Understanding Conflict

Figuring out what happens to cause a conflict, that there are two sides to a conflict (not just one's own), and that each side plays a role in causing the conflict are essential aspects of learning to manage conflict. In *Best Day of the Week*, Angela and Calvin, like all children, are learning about conflict and what causes it by directly experiencing it.

To develop the attitudes and skills of a positive conflict resolver, children need help from adults and lots of practice having positive conflict-resolving experiences. And, before they can even begin to think about positive solutions to conflicts, children have to learn to understand their conflicts and the problems that create them.

Perspective Taking

Young children have a very hard time understanding that there is more than one side to a conflict. Their minds are often filled with their own needs and desires, which makes it hard to see that someone else's view might be different. Angela and Calvin show us this when they each have a different idea about what to play with the card table—store or pirates.

Learning how to understand someone else's point of view is a long, slow process, but it is one of the essential abilities in positive conflict resolution. Calvin and Angela's conflict can help children learn about different perspectives. Their conflict begins with two clearly stated and separate points of view (to play store or pirates), which they gradually succeed at blending into a single positive solution (a store where the pirates come to buy supplies).

Recognizing Feelings

To resolve conflicts peacefully, people need to be able to recognize their own feelings as well as the feelings of others, and they must learn to care about how other people feel. Often adults try to help children deal with their feelings simply by teaching them to label their feelings. But understanding feelings is a dynamic process involving self-awareness and cognitive complexity. It involves figuring out what contributed to certain feelings and then connecting those feelings to actions and situations (for example, knowing what happened to cause a child to feel the way she does). Helping children deal with their feelings also involves knowing what people can do to help their feelings change.

Young children need help to understand and learn how to express their own feelings; they need even more help learning to empathize with others. Knowing that the feelings they share in the classroom will be respected is a necessary prerequisite. Only then will children be able to openly express how they feel using vehicles such as play, drawings, and words.

Children begin to understand the feelings of others first by recognizing concrete, tangible manifestations of feelings, like facial expressions and specific actions. This recognition helps them begin to feel someone else's emotions; then they can try to figure out what to do.

Throughout *Best Day of the Week*, Angela and Calvin's feelings are conveyed in terms young children can understand—by how their faces look. When angry, Calvin's eyes get "sharp" and Angela's face gets hot; Calvin grins and his eyes widen when he feels good.

Escalation

A conflict gets worse as people say and do things that make it heat up, or escalate. Learning what makes a conflict get worse is an essential part of conflict resolution, but that can be very hard for young children to understand. It involves relating several ideas, such as how your words and actions affect others.

In *Best Day of the Week*, we see Calvin and Angela's conflict get worse (escalate) before it gets better because of the things they say to each other. Escalating may include put-downs, bias statements, and physical fighting.

Put-Downs

Put-downs are critical, mean, or rejecting remarks that usually hurt feelings and almost always escalate conflict. In *Best Day of the Week*, Angela and Calvin both escalate the conflict with put-downs. Calvin calls Angela's game of store "a dumb game," and Angela calls Calvin's beloved pirate play "a stupid game."

Young children frequently hear put-downs from their peers, from brothers and sisters, and from media that is rife with put-downs and disrespectful language. When adults hear children using put-downs, they often say, "You shouldn't say that," or "It's not nice to say that." But many children do not understand the full meaning of their put-downs or their effects on others.

Best Day of the Week gives teachers a chance to bring put-down language into the open for discussion and to help children begin to make sense of put-downs. Children need to examine put-down comments with the help of adults. They need to talk about such issues as what is meant by the put-down they use, why people use put-downs, how put-downs make other people feel, and how put-downs escalate conflict.

Put-downs have a special power for young children who are just learning that what they say can have an effect on someone else. They like to experiment with the effects put-downs can have, but they need help understanding how this actually feels to someone else. Teachers can capitalize on the fascination young children have with put-downs to help the children understand how they affect others. Discussions about put-downs can gradually teach children a whole range of ways to have positive instead of negative effects on others.

Bias Statements

Bias statements are put-downs that refer to aspects of personal identity, such as gender, race, culture, age, or socioeconomic status. In *Best Day of the Week*, when Calvin says, "You're a stupid girl!" to Angela, he puts down Angela's gender as part of his insult. Even though young children do not understand bias statements in the same way as adults, they can still use them in negative ways and can feel the pain of a put-down when it is directed at them.

Children gradually construct an understanding of the abstract and complex concepts of gender and sexism, race and racism, class and classism, and other "isms." What they learn is influenced by their level of development, their experience, and the many forms of "isms" they are exposed to in the society in which they are growing up.

Children hear bias statements and use them when they are angry in the same way that they use other put-down statements. Only gradually do children come to understand that bias statements are a particular kind of put-down that negatively refers not only to one other person but to the identity of a whole group of people.

Because of their egocentrism, children are capable of making bias comments without realizing how they make others feel. And because they tend to focus on one thing at a time, children can forget all the other qualities of another person while they are delivering a put-down. All in all, the way young children think can make their bias statements seem especially thoughtless and mean.

Within this complex mixture of developmental and experiential influences, it is hard to know what any one child fully means by a bias statement made in a given moment. With all these complexities in mind, teachers can explore with children the meanings behind their bias statements, with the goal of helping children gradually understand more about how these comments hurt and what bias statements really mean. Through this process, children will be learning creative conflict resolution and a greater appreciation and respect for diversity.

Teachers also can help children learn more sensitive and productive ways to express negative feelings without using put-downs or bias statements. A teacher who heard Calvin say to Angela, "You're a dumb girl," might be tempted to respond, "Don't say that, Calvin. It's wrong to call Angela a dumb girl." But it would be more helpful to Calvin to explore what's behind the comment and why he said it, and to help him find a more respectful way to voice his frustration over Angela's unwillingness to play his pirate game.

Active listening and open-ended questions can help teachers and children do this. In this situation, for example, the teacher might have said to Calvin: "I can tell from what you said that you're feeling really mad at Angela right now. Look at Angela's face—she's feeling really bad too. Let's see if we can come up with some words to tell each other how we feel that don't hurt. Do you have any ideas?"

Physical Fighting

While Calvin and Angela solve their problem with words alone, many conflicts among young children quickly escalate to the point of physical fighting. It is hard for young children to control their impulses (the way Angela did when Calvin called her a "stupid girl") and to imagine effective alternatives to physical fighting, especially in the heat of the moment. Children are susceptible to physical fighting because it is the most concrete, immediate, and seemingly powerful solution they have available. And it is an approach children commonly see—in the media and, for many children, in other parts of their lives as well.

While Calvin and Angela do not resort to physical fighting, teachers can use *Best Day of the Week* to teach alternatives to physical fighting by talking about what would happen if their conflict did lead to a physical fight and why it did not.

De-Escalation

It takes much more skill and experience to de-escalate a conflict and work toward a peaceful resolution than it does to escalate it. De-escalating a conflict requires capabilities that are difficult for young children, such as perspective taking, dynamic thinking, and the ability to relate ideas logically. De-escalation also requires children to develop and use impulse control to stop what they are doing, delay getting their immediate needs met, and shift to a different approach. To do this requires controlling one's anger, which is hard for everyone, but it is especially hard for young children.

In addition to the capabilities just described, most children also need a lot of experience before they can trust that this shift from escalation to de-escalation can lead to a positive solution for them. In *Best Day of the Week*, Angela shows impulse control and an impressive level of experience and trust when she wants to tell Calvin that he is a dumb and stupid boy but manages to stop and say how she feels ("I don't like it when you call me a stupid girl"). The conflict de-escalates as a result of using "I" statements and active listening.

"I" Statements

When Angela says, "I don't like it when you call me a stupid girl," she is using an "I" statement. An "I" statement is an expression of what someone feels or needs that doesn't cast blame on another person. "I" statements often de-escalate conflict and, in this conflict, Angela's "I" statement begins the process.

"I" statements are especially challenging for young children, who usually think about only one thing at a time and can have problems making causal connections. Making an "I" statement requires children to identify and talk about their feelings and make connections between their feelings and a situation. For example, in *Best Day of the Week*, Angela is able to identify her feelings of being hurt, and she makes a causal connection between her feelings and the situation (she is hurt because Calvin put her down). Angela is then able to constructively talk about her feelings when she uses an "I" statement to tell Calvin, "I don't like it when you call me a stupid girl."

Active Listening

Listening with full attention to another person and showing in some tangible way that you have heard and understood what has been said is another skill that can help to de-escalate conflict. As children see that their comments have been heard, they begin to trust that their needs can be met. We see Calvin actively listening to Angela's suggestion that they solve their problem by playing store and pirates at the same time when he asks, "You mean we have the pirates come to the store?"

Active listening is a lot harder than it looks. It requires a sense of personal security and the ability to suspend one's own concerns long enough to hear someone else's concerns. Beyond this, active listening requires that we create meaning from what we have heard and are then able to show that we have understood it.

Learning the skills of active listening is a long, slow developmental process that young children can begin, with a teacher's help. As children practice active listening skills, they usually begin to feel the power of the conflict resolution process and realize that positive solutions are possible.

We have found it interesting that, from a developmental perspective, active listening often is a more difficult challenge for young children than making "I" statements. Active listening involves understanding someone else's point of view, while "I" statements are an expression of a child's own point of view.

Finding Solutions

The goal of positive conflict resolution is to find a solution everyone can agree to—a win-win solution—like Calvin and Angela do when they discover that they can play store and pirates at the same time. This is different from a win-lose solution, which we see them exploring earlier in the story when Calvin suggests they play pirates first and store after that, and Angela suggests they play store first and pirates later. We do not see a lose-lose solution in the story, but Calvin and Angela could have ended up physically fighting or going home angry and not playing with the table at all.

Win-win is really a way of being together in the classroom. It is an approach to conflicts between children, between the teacher and a child, or between the teacher and a group of children that includes all of the participants. It's an approach that involves agreement between everyone involved. It means not imposing a solution on others to which they did not agree.

It can be very hard for teachers to get comfortable with the win-win approach. To use it with confidence takes time, experience, and lots of support. It also involves a willingness to share power with children and truly value their ideas. The issue of power sharing is discussed more fully in chapter 8.

The win-win approach is difficult for young children, too, but for different reasons. They have difficulty thinking about a solution that would work for both sides in a conflict because egocentric and static thinking get in their way. It is also hard for young children to imagine how solutions will work in practice before they have had the chance to experience them directly.

On their own, young children will come up with more lose-lose and win-lose solutions to conflict than win-win solutions. These are the solutions they see modeled, especially in the media and the culture at large. They also are the solutions that require the least amount of skill from a young child trying to satisfy egocentric needs. But, with the teacher's help, children can begin to experience the greater gain that can come from finding win-win solutions to their conflicts.

Summary of the Skills and Concepts Underlying Conflict Resolution

Understanding Conflict: Learning about the nature of conflict, its causes, and what it means for the people involved in it.

> Perspective Taking: Learning how to understand someone else's point of view.

> Recognizing Feelings: Understanding one's own feelings as well as the feelings of others.

Escalation: What people do to make a conflict get worse.

> Put-Downs: Critical, mean, or rejecting remarks that hurt feelings.

> Bias Statements: Put-downs that refer to aspects of a person's identity, such as gender or race.

> Physical Fighting: Any form of hostile physical contact, such as hitting or kicking.

De-Escalation: What people can do to reduce conflict.

> "I" Statement: An expression of what a person feels or needs without casting blame on another person.

> Active Listening: Listening with full attention to another person and showing in some tangible way that you have heard and understand what has been said.

Finding Solutions: Learning about the nature of solutions to conflicts and how they work for the people involved.

> Win-Win Solutions: A solution that satisfies both or all of the sides involved in the conflict.

> Win-Lose Solutions: A solution where one side of the conflict prevails over the other.

> Lose-Lose Solutions: A solution where everyone involved in the conflict does *not* get what they want.

PART 2

Teaching Conflict Resolution with
Best Day of the Week

CHAPTER 4

Skills and Ideas Embedded in *Best Day of the Week*

Best Day of the Week portrays the kind of conflict young children might actually have in a way that they can understand. Angela and Calvin's adventure leads to a conflict that is common among young children when two points of view collide. Embedded in the story are the many skills and concepts discussed in the last chapter. As Angela and Calvin work through their conflict, they demonstrate the kinds of skills children can use to peacefully resolve their own conflicts. Let's look at the story to see how the skills and concepts of conflict resolution are embedded within it.

Best Day of the Week

STORY

Calvin woke up when he heard his brother cough in the crib next to him. Their bedroom was still dark, but Calvin could tell by the noises outside on the street that it was morning.
Calvin felt tired. He didn't want to get up.
Then he remembered what day it was.
Thursday. The best day of the week.
The day everyone in the neighborhood put out their trash.

COMMENTARY

Right from the start, children see Calvin as having experiences like their own, which will include a conflict with a friend as the story continues.

Best Day of the Week

STORY	COMMENTARY
The day that people put things they didn't want anymore out on the sidewalk for the city trucks to pick up.	
The day Calvin might find something interesting to play with among the things people threw away.	
Like the old broken table leg he was using for a telescope when he played pirates.	Calvin has a passion for play and clear ideas about how to use materials for pretend, which could lead to conflict if a play-mate doesn't agree.
And the box full of Styrofoam pieces that Calvin and Angela pretended were pirates' treasure.	
Angela lived in the apartment next door to Calvin. She was his best friend.	
Every morning Angela and Calvin walked to school with Angela's big brother Hector.	It's because of this relationship that Calvin and Angela will get the opportunity to experience conflict and to work on conflict resolution together.
Hector was forever saying to Angela and Calvin, "Hurry up. Walk faster or we'll be late to school."	
But on Thursdays, Hector always made sure they left a little early so there would be time to look over the trash.	
As they left Calvin's house this Thursday morning, Calvin's mother walked with them to the front steps. "You can look at the things thrown away on the street," she said, "but don't you go pokin' around inside any trash bags. You understand?"	
Three heads nodded up and down. Calvin and Hector nodded slowly. Angela's head moved twice as fast. Calvin's mother smiled. "Have a wonderful day," she said.	

Best Day of the Week

STORY	COMMENTARY
The friends headed toward school but didn't spot anything very interesting for three blocks.	
Then, as they rounded the corner onto Center Street, Angela stopped and pointed.	
A square object stood between two trash barrels in front of a brick building.	
Getting closer, they realized that the square object was a folded card table—with only one leg bent and just a few scrapes on the top.	
Angela examined the table, then announced, "We can play with this after school!"	
"How are we going to keep it until then?" Calvin asked. But Hector was already pulling the table out from between the two barrels.	Hector, Angela, and Calvin show us skills children need for constructive social relationships: interacting, listening to each other, and working together.
Hector guided the card table toward a narrow space between two buildings. Then they all pushed the table into the alleyway.	
Hector gave the table an extra nudge to get it fully out of view.	
All day in school Calvin thought about the card table. He thought about how he could throw a blanket over it and make it into a perfect pirates' cave.	The potential for conflict begins when Calvin and Angela begin to form different *perspectives* about how to play with the card table.
Angela thought about the card table all day too. She thought about how she could put a blanket over it and make it into a perfect place to play store.	
Calvin thought, "I'll hide in the pirates' cave and spy on the bad pirates."	The two different *points of view* are solidifying.

Best Day of the Week

STORY	COMMENTARY

Angela thought, "I'll get some paper and scissors and make signs to put in my store."

Hector, Angela, and Calvin nearly ran out of school to the spot where they'd hidden the card table. Three pairs of eyes peered into the dark alley. The card table leaned against the brick wall. Exactly as they had left it.

Angela and Calvin dragged the table into Calvin's apartment and into his room. They called out the window to Hector, "We got it to stand up!" Hector waved to them as he walked down the street to meet the big kids.

Angela and Calvin got a blanket and threw it over the top of the table. They peered into the dark space underneath.
It was all closed up.
A perfect place to play.

Then, at the exact same moment, Calvin and Angela both spoke:

"Let's get the pirate treasure and play pirates," said Calvin.
"Let's put all kinds of stuff in it and play store," said Angela.

Their two different *perspectives* suddenly collide.

Best Day of the Week

STORY	COMMENTARY

Calvin looked at Angela.
Angela looked at Calvin.

"You always want to play store," Calvin said.
"Let's play pirates."

"Pirates is all you ever want to play," said Angela.
"I want to play store."

Calvin's eyes got sharp. "But there are no bad guys in store," he said. "It's a dumb game."

Calvin makes a put-down statement and the conflict escalates.

Angela's eyes got dark. "Well, pirates isn't fun for me," she said. "It's a stupid game."

Angela makes a put-down statement and the conflict continues to escalate.

Calvin's mouth got small and thin. He said, "Store is a stupid girls' game. And you're a stupid girl."

Calvin makes a bias statement and the conflict escalates once again.

Angela felt her face get hot.

She opened her mouth. She wanted to tell Calvin that he was a dumb and stupid boy. But she stopped.

Angela considers making a bias statement, but she stops herself.

She looked at Calvin.
She could still hear Calvin's mean words.

Angela felt hurt.
She was quiet.

Angela identifies her feelings.

Then Angela said, "I don't like it when you call me a stupid girl."

Angela makes an "I" statement and begins the process of de-escalation.

Calvin looked at Angela.
Her face was sad.

Calvin felt confused.

Best Day of the Week

STORY	COMMENTARY
He was still mad, but he felt bad too. And he still wanted to play pirates.	Calvin identifies his *feelings*.
Calvin said, "I'll let you use my telescope if you'll play pirates."	Calvin begins trying to find a positive *solution* to the conflict.
Angela shook her head no.	
Calvin tried another idea: "Why don't we play pirates first and then play store after that?"	Calvin suggests a *win-lose solution*.
Angela didn't want to play pirates first. "We could play store first and then play pirates later," she said.	Angela suggests a different *win-lose solution*.
Calvin made a nasty face.	
Angela looked away into the dark cozy space under the table. Right at that moment an idea burst into her mind.	
"I know what," she said. "We can play store and the pirates can come to the store and buy all the stuff they need for their ship!"	Angela suggests a *win-win solution*.
Calvin's brown eyes widened. "You mean we have the pirates come to the store?"	Calvin shows that he is *actively listening* to Angela's idea.
A grin spread across his face.	
Calvin ran for the box of Styrofoam pieces he was using for pirate treasure. "The pirates can use this for money," he said. "Just the good pirates, though. We'll hide it from the bad pirates."	
Angela grabbed paper from her school bag and began drawing a map. She drew lines and added some circles and put X's inside them. She handed her map to Calvin.	
"Yes!" shouted Calvin. "This is how the pirates can find our store!"	

Connecting Children to Important Themes

The content of *Best Day of the Week* reflects several themes important in the lives of children growing up today. The hope is that these themes will resonate with children in ways that have meaning for them and relate to their understanding of the world. The book also offers you a vehicle for connecting with children around these important themes:

Cross-Cultural Friendships. Children need to see themselves reflected in the images around them. And they need a chance to see how people from diverse backgrounds can work out their conflicts together and still be close friends. By having Angela and Calvin be from different cultural groups, *Best Day of the Week* presents children with a meaningful example. It also provides a resource to use that models appreciation and respect for racial and cultural diversity.

Good and Bad Pirates. Good guy/bad guy play has an appeal to children, especially boys, because it resonates with developmental concerns such as good versus bad, right over wrong, feelings of empowerment, and gender identity. Popular media and toys offer children "bad guy" characters in excess, and these almost always involve violence. Teachers describe how children often repetitively imitate the violence of such characters. The kind of characters children need for their play should allow children to address developmental issues in ways that meet their needs but do not connect these developmental issues so strongly with violence.

The pirate theme in *Best Day of the Week* offers children an opportunity to work on their developmental issues in ways that allow their own meanings and creativity to enter the play, making it more likely that their play will serve as a vehicle for making sense of their own experience and for growth.

Friendships Between Girls and Boys. Calvin's interest in playing pirates and Angela's in playing store are common gender differences found in children's play. Popular media and toys today amplify and make these gender differences rigid, and according to teachers, are leading to less play between girls and boys in the classroom.

By having Angela and Calvin as best friends and showing how they find common ground for playing together, *Best Day of the Week* can help to break down some of the gender stereotypes that are on the rise in early childhood classrooms. The kind of communication and dialogue that Calvin and

Angela have can show children how to bring their separate interests into their cooperative play. Angela invents an inclusive solution when she suggests merging the two games. This can help children see how they can maintain their separate interests and identities as they find ways to play together.

Recycled Toys. As children's play has become more and more dependent on commercial toys, many children have begun to think that they need to buy the "right" toy in order to play. *Best Day of the Week* tells a story about two children who enjoy using various materials as props in their play.

The focus on using these materials rather than commercial toys encourages children to bring their own purposes and meanings to their play. It also de-emphasizes the importance of having money to be able to play, provides a model for environmental responsibility, and minimizes some of the negative social messages embedded in commercial toys.

An Urban Adventure Story. Many teachers working on conflict resolution in urban areas have been asking for material to use with young children. *Best Day of the Week* tells a story about children who are living resourcefully and creatively in the city. Children who live in urban areas will be able to see themselves reflected on these pages. And children who live in other settings will be exposed to a different way of life where children still share many concerns similar to their own.

CHAPTER 5

Using *Best Day of the Week* to Talk About Conflict Resolution

Best Day of the Week can be used as the starting point for teaching the conflict resolution concepts and skills described in chapter 3, as well as for infusing these ideas into the total classroom curriculum. In this chapter, we take you through a series of activities that illustrate how this process might occur. We call these suggestions "starting points" because, when working well, they will evolve and change as you bring in the specific needs and input of the children.

Learning Conflict Resolution Skills

Children learn conflict resolution skills best when:

> They can interact with the skills and ideas in an active way.
>
> They can practice their developing skills and ideas in a variety of situations.
>
> They can relate their own experiences to these new ideas and skills.
>
> They can bring their whole cultural identity into the learning process.
>
> The skills and ideas relate closely to children's developmental understandings.
>
> The entire classroom is a living example of creative conflict resolution in a peaceful and just environment.

Introducing *Best Day of the Week*

Here are suggestions for three ways to read *Best Day of the Week* to children:

1. Initiate a discussion before reading the story to prepare the children to connect the story to their own lives.
2. Read the entire story and then have a discussion.
3. Read up to the point where conflict occurs in the story, then stop to ask the children what they think will happen next.

1. Initiate a discussion before reading the story.

Before you begin reading *Best Day of the Week*, you might want to initiate a discussion with the children to help them connect the story to their own lives.[2] You might tell them a story about a conflict you have had in your life or about some other aspect of the book that relates to your experience. You can also ask open-ended questions that help the children connect the story to their own lives:

- Have you ever had a conflict with someone? Tell us about that.
- What happened?
- What did you do?
- Can you think of anything else you could have done in that situation?

2. Read the entire story, then lead a discussion.

Read the story all the way through, then lead a discussion by asking open-ended questions. You can also ask questions that help the children connect the story to their own lives (see above). The following questions are designed to help children make sense of the story for themselves and express their diverse ideas about it:

- What happened in the story?
- What do you think about Angela and Calvin's conflict?
- Why do you think it happened?
- How did Angela feel? How did Calvin feel?
- How did they figure out what to do?
- What do you think about how they solved their conflict?
- What would you have done if you were Calvin? What would you have done if you were Angela?

---

2. For more information about using this kind of an approach, see Voices of Love and Freedom: A K-12 Multicultural Literature, Ethics, and Prevention Program (Family, Friends, and Community, Judge Baker Children's Center, 295 Longwood Avenue, Boston, MA 02115.)

Guidelines for Leading Discussions

- Ask open-ended questions.
- Get comments and ideas from many children before moving on to the next question.
- Create an atmosphere where children feel safe to express diverse ideas and opinions.

3. Discuss the story while reading it.

Read the story up to the point where Angela and Calvin say at the same time what game they want to play. Stop reading and ask questions about what is happening, then have children predict what will happen next. With this approach, you encourage the children to think about Angela and Calvin's conflict before they know how the story will end. Ask such questions as the following:

- Uh-oh! What's happening here?
- How do you think Calvin is feeling?
- How is Angela feeling?
- What do you think is going to happen next?
- Do you think they can figure this out? How?
- What do you think Angela should do? What do you think Calvin should do?

After you finish reading the story, talk about what actually did happen, using the open-ended questions listed for the second approach.

Extending the Story

To help children connect the story to their lives and begin to build the foundations for using the conflict resolution skills in it, bring the story into other parts of the classroom curriculum.

Dramatic Play

Children can play out the story in the dramatic play area. Translating stories from books into dramatic "retellings" with children's own unique variations will help children make sense of a story for themselves. This active "retelling" of a story also strengthens literacy skills, since it gives children a deeper understanding of the story. Some props to put out might include:

- A table with a cloth thrown over it (for store or pirate cave)
- A table leg or long cardboard tube (for the telescope)
- A box of Styrofoam pieces (for treasure or money)
- Paper and markers (for drawing treasure maps and store signs)
- Other pirate and store props such as eye patches and a cash register

The Importance of Play

Play is one of the central ways children work out their understanding of new experiences. Through using their creativity, imagination, and problem-solving abilities in play, children actively remake their experiences in personally meaningful ways.

Best Day of the Week can be a springboard to rich and creative play for children. They can try some of the play ideas Angela and Calvin think of such as playing pirate and store. Reenacting the conflict aspects of the story through play can also enhance children's learning about conflict and conflict resolution.

Some children may need special help "playing out" *Best Day of the Week* and other stories you read to them. Many children today have difficulty beginning and sustaining their play. With so much TV watching and too little time for play, and with highly realistic TV-based toys that limit rather than expand children's play, many children have difficulty playing in creative and personally meaningful ways. Sometimes their play looks more like imitations of TV scripts than their own original productions. And often it is fraught with violence children imitate from the screen.

You can facilitate children's play using *Best Day of the Week*. Helping children role-play this story can help them develop better play skills in general and more creative toy use, as well as further their understanding of conflict resolution in ways that have meaning for them.

For a more detailed discussion of the factors that undermine children's play and promote violent play themes, see Nancy Carlsson-Paige and Diane E. Levin's *Who's Calling the Shots? How to Respond Effectively to Children's Fascination with War Play, War Toys, and Violent TV* (Gabriola Island, BC, Can.: New Society, 1990) and *The War Play Dilemma: Balancing Needs and Values in the Early Childhood Classroom* (New York: Teachers College, 1987).

Facilitating Play

To facilitate children's play using a story you can do the following:

- Help them get started by suggesting a specific role or situation.
- Watch the play so you know what's going on and can offer suggestions to help children extend it.
- Help children plan their play (for instance, by asking questions such as, "What will you need to play pirate?" "What could you use for treasure?").
- Offer generic, multipurpose props that children can use in ways of their own choosing.
- Talk to children about their play to help them reflect and build onto what they have done.
- Encourage older or more experienced players ("play mentors") to play with younger or less experienced players.
- Ask children to share what they do in their play at class meetings. This can give ideas to other children for their own play.
- Help children draw pictures and write down their stories. You can share these at class meetings too.

If this is an approach you and the children like, select other books involving conflict to dramatize in play (for instance, *The Butter Battle Book* by Dr. Seuss, *Matthew and Tilly* by Rebecca C. Jones, and other books listed in chapter 9). The more you do this, the more skills the children will develop as players and in dramatic reenactments of conflict stories.

Solving Classroom Conflicts

You can extend discussions about conflict in the story to conflicts that come up in the classroom.

Drawings and Stories. Suggest that children draw pictures and write stories about a current conflict or other conflicts they have had. These drawings can be shared at class meetings, and together you can build up a broader base of experience about conflicts and how to resolve them.

See figures 1, 2 and 3 on the following page.

Figure 1
"We were yelling at each other and then my mother came and told us we had to share. Then we stopped yelling at each other and started to share." [Second grade]

Figure 2
"We're crying because we were pulling the doll and it broke. We ran and told our mother and we were talking all at once and our mother said, 'I can't understand what you're saying.' And then we ran to our father and started talking at the same time again. And then our father sent us to our rooms to figure it out ourselves." [Second grade]

Figure 3
"I was drawing my picture. When I was finished I said, 'This picture is beautiful.' Kim said, 'It doesn't look beautiful without any purple.'" [Kindergarten]

Puppets. Another idea is to make simple stick puppets of Angela and Calvin to use for reenacting the story. (See the puppet cut-outs of Calvin and Angela at the end of this book.) These puppets can be used at class meetings. Hold a puppet in each hand and use them to talk the children through the conflict, encouraging the children to contribute their ideas to Calvin and Angela. Ask questions like:

- What can Angela say right now?
- How do you think Angela and Calvin are feeling?
- Do you want to give Calvin or Angela an idea for how to solve the problem and see what they both think?

Using puppets can assist the children in working on many aspects of conflict and creates a way for you to model conflict resolution skills. Gradually you can have children hold and work the puppets as you lead the discussion. Once children have become familiar with using them, place the puppets in a special area of the classroom where children can use them to create their own reenactments of conflicts and other events. See chapter 9 for a more detailed discussion of using puppets in a conflict resolution curriculum.

CHAPTER 6

Teaching Specific Skills: Conflicts and How They Get Worse

You can use *Best Day of the Week* to teach children specific conflict resolution skills. For example, focus on one skill, such as perspective taking. Use the story to introduce the idea at a class meeting, and then to extend activities throughout the curriculum.

Here are some ideas for beginning to teach specific skills. They will probably lead you and the children to many other ideas for how to work on these skills in your classroom.

Learning About Perspective Taking

The real challenge with an abstract concept like perspective taking is finding ways that young children can experience it in concrete and meaningful situations. To do this, help the children connect to other people's experiences in ways they can understand. For example, you can say, "Janey waited a really long time to use the truck, and it got too hard for her to wait." Then help the children see the connections between each person in the situation by saying, "Janey, when you took the truck Alex got mad, and so he grabbed it back."

Using *Best Day of the Week*

Read the story again and talk about Calvin and Angela as full characters—what they look like, where they live, what they like to do, and their friendship. Talk about Angela and Calvin's conflict and their different points of view—what they disagree about, what each of them want, how they express their different wants. Use the following activities to help children experience the point of view of both Calvin and Angela in concrete ways.

Point of View Feet. Cut the shape of two pairs of feet from paper and tape them to the floor. Have one child stand in each and act out the characters, then switch and do it again as the opposite character. With younger children who have trouble shifting points of view, have each child act out only one character. With older children, try having them change characters midstream.

Puppets. Make Calvin and Angela stick puppets, each with a happy face on one side and an unhappy face on the other. Read through the story and have two children turn the puppets to show how they think Calvin and Angela are reacting. Younger children may need your help, while the older children might want to try to manipulate both puppets at once, coordinating both points of view on their own. See chapter 9 for a more detailed discussion of using puppets in a conflict resolution curriculum.

Building Perspective Taking into the Curriculum

Use situations that arise spontaneously in the classroom to focus on point of view. For example, if two children are playing with blocks and each has a different idea of what to build, use this moment to point out that each has a different point of view. Bring these examples to class meetings. Ask the children to find examples in their day when they see different points of view. Use puppets at class meetings to act out situations and stories, showing how each puppet sees the same thing differently. Also practice taking perspective in the classroom using these concrete and experiential activities:

Feeling Photos. A central part of understanding someone else's perspective is recognizing the feelings that go with that perspective. Photographs of faces expressing a wide range of feelings will help children recognize the feelings that go with a particular point of view. You can use feeling photos to talk about how someone is feeling and help children think about the other person's situation and point of view. For more on feeling photos, see chapter 9 and the "Learning About Feelings" section below.

Blocks. Have one child make a building with a set of four to six assorted blocks and then have another child try to copy it using a matching set of blocks. Have the children switch roles. (This is fun to do with other kinds of materials too.) Encourage the children to talk about what they are doing. Older children can do this activity sitting back-to-back, each with one set of blocks. Have one child build a structure and then describe it to the other, who tries to copy it without looking. When they think they are done, have the children look at the two buildings and talk about what they see. Then have them switch roles and try again. Copying another child's block pattern is one way to teach children to take perspective.

Games. Play games that have children look at objects from different points of view and describe what they see. For example, a house made with building blocks can have different numbers of windows and doors visible from various angles.

Mystery Objects. Put an object in a sock and encourage the children to guess what is inside. Ask them to talk about how they came up with their guesses. Point out how children have very different ideas (perspectives) about the mystery object.

Stories. Try reading other stories where characters have different points of view. (See chapter 9 for a list of books.) Use the puppets and the point of view feet to play with this idea, letting the children "stand in the shoes" of different characters. With older children, read the conventional story of *The Three Pigs* and talk about it from the pigs' point of view. Then read *The True Story of the Three Little Pigs by A. Wolf*, which presents the same story from the wolf's point of view. Talk about the wolf's point of view and the idea that there often is more than one point of view in the same situation. You can use the two versions of the three little pigs story as a model for looking at points of view in other popular stories in books and media. Try having children retell the stories from various characters' points of view.

Connecting Perspective Taking Skills to Children's Conflicts

After conflicts have occurred among children and emotions have subsided, help children look at the conflict from both points of view. Try rephrasing the problem for the children by restating both perspectives. For example, you can say, "Jenna, you wanted to sit next to Kimberly, but Marcus was already sitting in this chair, and he wanted to stay there." Ask older children to draw pictures of their own and the other point of view. If they agree to it, share these pictures with the whole group at a class meeting.

Have children talk about conflicts they have in their own lives. After they have had time to describe the problem from their own point of view, encourage them to imagine it from the other person's perspective. The point of view feet, puppets, or other tools we have described can help them do this. Be sure to respect children's ideas, and don't make them feel that there is one thing they should say or feel.

Learning about Feelings

Young children base most of their ideas on concrete experiences. Having them focus on feelings in the conflicts they experience can help them learn about their own feelings and how feelings are related to actions. For instance, you can say, "Tell me how you felt when you had to wait so long for a turn."

Making the feelings of others as connected to concrete and meaningful experience as possible can also help children learn about how others feel. For example, you can ask, "How do you think Javier is feeling right now? How can you tell?" Helping children relate to the feelings of others can help children develop feelings of care and empathy. For instance, you can ask, "Have you ever felt that way?"

Using *Best Day of the Week*

You can use *Best Day of the Week* as a starting point for focusing on feelings. Go through the story and use Calvin and Angela to talk about feelings. Try talking about how each character feels at various points and what caused that feeling by asking:

- How did Angela feel when Calvin wanted to play pirates first?
- What made her feel that way?
- How did Calvin feel when Angela called pirates a "stupid game"?

Also discuss how Angela's and Calvin's feelings interact with each other by asking:

- How was Calvin feeling when he called Angela a "stupid girl"?
- How did Angela feel when Calvin called her a "stupid girl"?
- How did Calvin feel when Angela made a sad face?

As the children talk about Calvin and Angela's feelings, help them connect their ideas to their own experiences. Ask children questions such as the following:

- Have you ever felt angry like Angela and Calvin did?
- What made you feel like that? What did you do?

Feeling Lists. Make a list of all the ways Angela and Calvin feel throughout the story. Include a variety of words for feelings. Have the children brainstorm for more words they can add to the list. Keep adding to it over time as new ideas come up. For children who can read and write, post the list in a convenient spot and have them add new words to it. In class discussions, draw on some of these words by asking, "Can you find anything on our 'feeling list' to describe how you feel right now?"

Building Feeling Activities into the Curriculum

You can help children recognize some of the complexities of their feelings. For instance, one teacher started using the term "blender feelings" to describe situations where children felt more than one way at the same time[3]. This happens in *Best Day of the Week* when Angela tells Calvin that she doesn't like it when he calls her a stupid girl. Calvin feels bad, mad, and confused, and he still wants to play with Angela.

Feeling Photos. To help younger children learn to recognize the concrete expressions of feelings and begin to talk about them, try using feeling photos—photos of faces expressing a wide range of feelings and representing a diversity of people. These photographs can be used in a variety of ways (see chapter 9 for further ideas). Ask questions like:

- How do you think this person is feeling?
- Why do you think they're feeling that way?
- Have you ever felt this way?
- Can you show us how your face looks when you feel this way? (Try having a mirror available for this.)

Learning How Conflicts Escalate

Even though the concept of conflict escalation (that people say and do things to worsen a conflict) requires complex thinking to understand, we can begin to work on this concept with young children in ways that are meaningful to them. A first step is for children to learn how their actions affect others. Although the causal connection between what a person does and how it affects others can be hard to grasp at first, with experience and practice in meaningful situations, children can learn to recognize escalation. This recognition, in turn, will develop their ability to successfully resolve conflicts.

---

3. *Thanks to Karen Economopoulos for showing us this idea and the power it can have with children.*

An important role for the teacher is to point out how a child's actions or words have affected another child. Younger children will primarily use actions to escalate conflict. This behavior can be made evident by asking such questions as, "Do you know what made Thomas smash your sand castle?"

As children get older, words become more important in conflict escalation. The teacher's role increasingly involves pointing out what has been said and its effects by asking such questions as, "Do you know what you said to make Maya say she's not your friend anymore?"

You can help children understand the idea of escalation by making it more concrete and experiential. Here are some activities to try:

Finding Conflict. Read the story and have children indicate in some way when they hear the conflict getting worse—for example, clapping their hands or tapping their feet. Go back and ask the children what specifically happened in the story to make them clap. This is an opportunity to start discussing put-downs and bias statements.

Escalation/De-Escalation Staircase. Build a staircase out of blocks and, as you are reading, move a small block (or other object) up the stairs each time the conflict escalates[4]. You can also move the object down the steps as the conflict de-escalates. If the children seem interested, use the escalation/de-escalation staircase with other conflicts from stories and their own experiences (see figures 5, 6a and 6b).

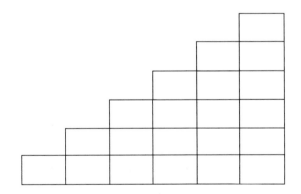

Figure 4: Escalation/De-Escalation Staircase

4. Thank you to William Kreidler for introducing us to his escalation/de-escalation staircase.

Figure 5
"George hit me in the hallway and I chased him. I said, 'I ain't your friend no more.' He said, 'I ain't yours either.' He pushed me. I hit him. The teachers stopped the fight. We had to go to the office." [First grade]

Figure 6a and 6b
"Me and my cousin were playin' in the snow. I pushed her. She pushed me. I pushed her back. I said, 'I'm goin' to school and I'm gettin' juice,' and she said, 'Get me some.' I said, 'I'm not, because you pushed me.' She said, 'I won't let you sleep in my bed no more when you spend the night.' Then my aunt came outside. My cousin said, 'She pushed me first.' And I said, 'She pushed me.' Then my aunt said, 'Go in the house now.' Later my cousin threw a snowball at me." [First grade]

Negative Endings. Let some of your discussions about conflict scenarios escalate. We found that children often want, even need, to explore conflicts that lead to physical fights and lose-lose endings.

Try retelling *Best Day of the Week* with a negative ending or letting children draw or tell an ending that results in a fight. Ask questions like:

- What happened that caused Calvin and Angela to fight?
- How do you think they feel about it?
- Have you had a fight like this with anyone?
- How did you feel about it?

Learning about Put-Downs and Bias Statements

Learning about put-downs and bias statements, which are key contributors to the escalation of conflicts, poses special challenges. For instance, young children are constructing an understanding of put-downs and bias statements by using their own experiences to figure out the meanings behind these kinds of comments. But most children have rarely had a chance to talk about them in an honest and safe way with adults or other children.

In addition, children's dichotomous thinking often leads them to think in stereotypes. The stereotypes they learn from the world around them fit easily with the way they think. The challenge for a constructivist teacher is to promote anti-bias attitudes that build meaningfully and gradually onto children's own ideas.

Using *Best Day of the Week*

Calvin and Angela's conflict offers a fairly safe starting point for talking about put-downs and bias statements. Each child's experience, culture, and development is different, so each child's ideas will be unique. First, try to understand what a child means when using put-downs and bias statements. Then you can base your response on the child's meaning and try to relate her ideas to the lessons about put-downs and bias statements you want to teach.

Try using these questions to learn more about children's understandings of put-downs and bias statements:

- What do you think about what Calvin and Angela were saying to each other when they got mad?
- Why do you think Calvin/Angela said that?
- What do you think about Calvin calling Angela a "stupid girl"?

- What do you think about when Angela said to Calvin that pirates is a "stupid game"?
- What happens when people say things like that?
- Has anyone ever said anything like that to you? Tell us about it. What did you do?

The following discussions provide examples of teachers using questions to learn more about children's understanding of put-downs and bias statements. They also illustrate the kinds of discussions to aim for when you work on conflict resolution skills with children. Throughout these discussions, the teachers were trying to:

- Encourage and respect all of the children's ideas
- Help children listen to one another
- Foster development through the exchange of ideas

CONVERSATION	COMMENTARY
Kindergarten	
Teacher: What did you think when Calvin said, "You're a stupid girl"?	These kindergarten children focus more on the power and meaning of the word *stupid* than on how the word affects Angela, which is a common way of thinking for five year olds.
Michael: It's not nice. That's a bad word.	They are using their own experience with "bad" words to try to understand the word *stupid*. They feel safe sharing their ideas about conflict with their teacher, who is listening for their meanings. Teachers never know what ideas might come up in discussions like this one.
Ernest: It's a swear.	
Michael: No, it isn't a swear. It's just a rude word.	
Ernest: It's a swear like *shit* and *fuck you*.	
Teacher: So you do know words like that...words that can make people mad.	

CONVERSATION	COMMENTARY
Teacher: What else do you think about what Calvin said? James: If you call a girl stupid, it means you don't like her. Chandra: I hate the person who said it to me, and I'm never gonna be her friend. Teacher: Yes, calling someone a mean word can make them not want to be your friend.	These five year olds are thinking about what the word *stupid* means to them by bringing in what they know. The teacher is beginning to help them focus on how put-downs affect them.
Teacher: When someone calls you something like what Calvin said, what do you do? Elena: When people call me stupid, I don't like it. I even want to push or hit them. Teacher: It makes you feel angry? Elena: Yes...and sad. Ben: When someone called me stupid, I almost pushed them.	These kindergartners are already aware of how put-downs make them want to fight back. They are beginning to understand the idea of escalation. The teacher is helping them talk about their feelings and connect them to what happens in a conflict.
Teacher: Why do you think Calvin told Angela she was a "stupid girl"? Owen: Because only girls like store. Teacher: Do only girls play store? Several Girls [in unison]: I like store! Teacher: Do any boys like to play store? Kao: I play store with my sister. Teacher: Let's set up a store in our classroom for both boys and girls to play in.	Owen may be referring to the story or to his own ideas about gender. The teacher probes to help clarify the children's thinking about gender and suggests an activity that boys and girls can enjoy together.

CONVERSATION	COMMENTARY
Teacher: Has anyone heard the word *put-down*? Maya: Yes, "put down" your paper.	Exploring children's meanings behind the words they use helps teachers stay close to children's understanding as they work on conflict resolution.
First and Second Grade Teacher: How do you think Angela felt when Calvin said, "You're a stupid girl"? Kayla: Mad, because he said girls were bad—girls can like to do a lot of different things, like play pirates. It hurt her feelings. Teacher: What do you think about that? Jackson: When he said that, she thought she lost her best friend because he called her stupid.	These second graders are aware of the feelings and thoughts that are beneath the surface of Angela and Calvin's conflict. They are thinking more logically about how behaviors affect others. Friendships become an important factor in conflict resolution for many second graders.
Teacher: What do you think about what Calvin said to Angela, "You're a stupid girl"? Eli: I think it was good of Angela to say she didn't like what he called her. Danisha: Well, Angela didn't say something back because she knew it would be bad and then it would get worse, and she still wanted to be his friend.	These first and second graders view Angela's reaction to Calvin's put-down positively. Angela's "I" statement ("I don't like it when you call me a stupid girl") is a model of how to speak out against bias statements.

CONVERSATION	COMMENTARY
Teacher: What happens when people say to each other things like what Calvin said? Leland: Someone calls me bad names, then someone says "your mother."	These second graders understand the power of put-downs and how they can be used to escalate conflict.
Teacher: What does that mean? Leslie: People just do that to cause fights. Leland: You don't like people to talk about your family.	Different put-downs have power and meaning for different children, which is something teachers need to hear about from the children they work with.
Teacher: Can you think of anything to do besides use mean words? Jamal: Stop...Ignore him...Just pretend he's not there.	Some children have a hard time figuring out positive alternatives to using put-downs or bias statements in their conflicts.
Teacher [*Talking with a child about the conflict drawing he made (see Figure 7)*]: Tell me what's happening in your drawing. José: This guy has two more friends trying to get this guy mad. Teacher: Why do they want to get him mad? José: 'Cause he has a different kind of mouth like this [*points to picture of figure's mouth with a zipper*], and they've got a mouth like this [*points to other figures' mouths with two lines*]. Teacher: So people get into fights because they don't look the same. [*Three other children rapidly contribute their ideas.*]	The teacher asks open-ended questions that help José talk about the meaning of his picture. She asks a question that helps him think about how the conflict in his picture started. This child is connecting differences in appearance to conflict escalation. Once differences in appearance was opened as a topic, many children had a lot to say about it. This discussion about bias is starting from the children's understanding of differences, a necessary starting point for work on bias.

Figure 7
"He has two friends helping him get the guy mad, 'cause he has an ugly face. He has a different kind of mouth part, like this [*pointing to the figure on the left with a 'zipper mouth'*]. And he's gonna say, 'Stupid!' And they have a mouth part like this [*pointing to the two figures on the right with two parallel lines for the mouth*]. And he says, 'Shut up!'" [Second Grade]

Connecting to Direct Experience

Bring an awareness of the children's own use of put-downs into the classroom.

Lists. Ask children about the put-downs that come from their experience. Make a list of these (see below) and add to it. Be sure to focus on the put-downs and not who said them. Talk about how it feels to hear put-downs.

Put-Downs Children Use

- You're ugly!
- I ain't your friend.
- Your mother!
- You can't come to my birthday party.
- Shut up!
- Your whole generation.
- You sure are ugly!
- Stupid fat boy.
- I won't be your friend.
- I hate you!

Practice Put-Ups. Practice making some "put-ups" (positive, affirming statements) to help children see alternatives to put-downs[5]. You will see more about these in the section on de-escalation in the next chapter.

Puppets. Use hand or stick puppets at class meetings to act out simple conflicts that are similar to the conflicts children have in the classroom. Have the puppets make put-down statements to each other. Stop and ask the children for their ideas about what is said and how it feels to hear it.

Discuss TV Put-Downs. Talk to children about the put-downs they hear on television. Children learn a lot about put-down statements from what they see on television; many children's television programs, especially cartoons, are riddled with put-downs. As issues of physical violence take center stage in discussions about children's television, put-downs are often overlooked. But they convey to children a general acceptance of mean and hurtful conflict-escalating behaviors.

Bringing television put-downs into discussions that grow out of *Best Day of the Week* can provide children with an effective avenue for counteracting what they see on television. For older children, videotape a children's television program that uses a lot of put-downs. Show a segment of the program to the children. Ask them to raise their hands every time they hear a put-down. Pause the tape to talk about it.

---

5. *Thanks to the Resolving Conflict Creatively Program for this idea.*

CHAPTER 7

Teaching Specific Skills: Conflicts and How They Get Better

We can help children learn that not only do some words and actions make conflicts get worse, other words and actions can help conflicts get better. You can use *Best Day of the Week* as a springboard for teaching children the skills involved in de-escalation.

Learning How to De-Escalate Conflicts

Most young children are only beginning to have the impulse control they need to stop themselves when they are in the midst of a conflict and begin the de-escalation process. By using the following techniques, we have seen this ability gradually develop in young children so that, by the primary grades, some are able to stop a conflict, especially when they have some concrete tools to help them.

Using *Best Day of the Week*

Using *Best Day of the Week* as a starting point for talking about de-escalation, help children see when and how the conflict stopped escalating—that is, when Angela stopped herself from calling Calvin "a dumb and stupid boy." Ask the children:

- Why do you think Angela stopped and didn't call Calvin "a stupid boy"?
- What do you think would have happened if Angela had called Calvin "a stupid boy"?

Puppets. Here is another place where puppets can help with the discussion. Try using simple sock puppets that represent Calvin and Angela, or use the cut-outs of them provided at the end of this guide. The puppets can act out the various scenarios the children think could have happened. Puppets provide a safe way for children to work out how various negative scenarios might have unfolded. Children may bring up physical fighting in this discussion, and you can help them safely explore their ideas about this. Point out how Angela stopped herself, and ask children what they think about this.

Connecting to Direct Experience

Children can talk about times when they have stopped themselves from making a conflict worse. Try asking, "What do you do to try to stop yourself when you're getting really mad?"

Lists. Start a list of things children have tried to cool down a conflict, and add to it as they come up with new ideas. Here are lists of "cool downs" and "put-ups" children came up with in such a discussion.

Cool Downs—What I've done to stop a conflict:

Kindergartners and First Graders

- I say, "Don't punch."
- I say, "Let's be friends."
- You can say, "Stop!" but sometimes they don't.
- I said, "Could I have a turn and then you have a turn?"
- Tell the other person to share.
- Tell them to stop.
- I said, "Let's talk it out."
- I said, "Let's trade seats so we can sit next to each other."
- I said, "If you don't stop fighting, you won't sit next to me."
- I get my father. Then my sister says, "I'll get my mommy."

Second and Third Graders

- I went into the house and played with my little sister instead.
- I said, "Give me my ball, because I'm going in the house since you don't want to share."
- I said, "Let's play something else, maybe that will be better."
- I wanted to fight, but I said, "Don't pick on my cousin."
- I said, "You have to share. It's one ball, not two balls."
- I said, "Why don't we just play Barbie, both of us together?"
- I said, "Well, can you be nice to me?" And she said, "Well, if you don't be mean to me, I won't be mean to you."
- I said, "Look, I don't want to fight. Let's talk it out."
- I said, "We shouldn't fight like this."
- I said, "One person gets a turn for three minutes, then the other."
- We had a fight over my yo-yo. One used it from nine to ten, then another from ten to eleven.
- I said to my sister, "I'll bring you to a movie sometime."
- I was mad so much that I didn't say anything. That stopped it.

"Put-Ups" Children Use

- Great job!
- I like your shirt.
- I like you.
- I like how you give me a thumbs-up.
- I like your picture.
- High five!
- You're nice!
- Want to play with me?
- You're my friend.

Stop Sign. Make a sign that says, "Stop—Think" on one side, and "Let's work it out" on the other[6]. This appeals to primary grade children, who are developing the ability to shift their thinking from one idea to another. The sign helps them to do this. You can use the sign when you are acting out or talking about conflicts at class meetings in order to make concrete the point when de-escalation begins. Put the sign in the conflict corner (see chapter 8).

Figure 8: "Stop—Think" and "Let's Work It Out" sign.

Learning to Use "I" Statements

"I" statements are learned best by children when they can practice them every day in the classroom and when teachers also use and model the skills. The following activities can help children develop the use of "I" statements.

Using *Best Day of the Week*

Reread Angela's "I" statement in *Best Day of the Week:* "I don't like it when you call me a stupid girl." Then ask, "Have you ever had a conflict where you said something that made things get better? What did you say?" Use puppets to act out what children say and to emphasize "I" statements.

---

6. *Thanks to William Kreidler for this idea.*

Connecting to Direct Experience

You can help younger children learn about "I" statements by helping them put into words what they wanted or needed in a conflict and how they felt. For example, you can say, "So you felt really mad when your sister took your stickers. You wanted them back."

When appropriate, you can reflect back to children what they say in the form of "I" statements. If a child says, for example, "I told my brother 'Don't mess up my game,'" you can say, "So your 'I' statement could be, 'I don't like it when you touch my game because I want to finish it.'"

When children are actually having conflicts in the classroom, try intervening and suggesting "I" statements. For instance, you can say, "So you're trying to tell Henry, 'I'm mad because I've been waiting so long to use that.'"

Lists. Try making a list of "I" statements that kids have or could use in the classroom.

Learning Active Listening

Active listening is best learned by children when they can see and use the skill throughout the day in authentic interactions with others. To help children begin to develop active listening skills in the classroom, consider the following suggestions:

- Strive to practice active listening yourself with children as much as possible throughout the day.
- Model active listening at class meetings by rephrasing what you hear children say. You can say, "So last night you played the hiding game with your mom and your brother and it was really fun!"
- Promote active listening in children's actual conflicts. For instance, you might say to a child, "What you're saying is, you would like Josh to let you use the funnel?"

Learning About Solutions to Conflict

Thinking of solutions to conflict is something young children really enjoy doing. We want to give children lots of experience thinking of solutions to conflict, choosing which ones to try, putting them into practice, and looking at how they worked. To do this, younger children will need a lot of help from the teacher. With age and experience, children will get better at finding win-win solutions to their conflicts without the teacher's help.

Using *Best Day of the Week*

Reread the story, stopping to discuss the different solutions that Calvin and Angela suggest to their conflict. Ask the children what they think about these different solutions. With win-lose solutions such as Calvin's idea ("Why don't we play pirates first and then play store after that?"), you can help the children think about the solution from both Angela's and Calvin's point of view. Have fun brainstorming solutions together. Ask the children:

- What do you think about these different solutions?
- Can you think up any other ideas for how Angela and Calvin might solve their problem?

Puppets. Puppets are very useful in helping children explore how both sides in a conflict need to like the idea for it to be a win-win solution. You can ask each puppet what it thinks of the solution. For instance, show how the Calvin puppet might like an idea, but how the Angela puppet might not like it. Explore lose-lose solutions too. Children will likely suggest some "fight and flight" scenarios, such as Angela and Calvin get more angry, get into a fist fight, stalk off and stop playing together. Ask questions like:

- What do you think about this?
- Have you had a conflict that ended up like this? Tell us about what happened.

Building Win-Win Solutions into the Classroom

Ask children if they have had any conflicts that ended in win-win solutions. Suggest looking for win-win solutions to conflicts that happen in the classroom. Discuss these at class meetings. Try keeping a list of the win-win solutions the children have found.

Books. Use other books to explore solutions to conflict. Make up win-win solutions for the conflicts in these books. With Dr. Seuss' *Butter Battle Book*, for example, you might ask, "How might the Yooks and the Zooks solve their problem without fighting?" Have children list several solutions that might work, as they do in the list that follows. Other books dealing with conflicts and conflict resolution are listed in chapter 9.

Solving the Yooks and Zooks' Problem

- Everybody can butter the bread on the top one day and on the bottom the next day.
- They can just do it any way they want.
- They can butter one piece on the top and one on the bottom and put them together to make a sandwich.
- They can put butter on all of the bread.

"The Yook and Zook are on a picnic. They are being friends."

Figure 9: One child's drawing of how the Yooks and Zooks can solve their conflict about whether butter should go on the top or the bottom of their bread.

Discuss TV Programming. This can be an effective time to bring up the television programs children watch. You can talk about how media figures solve their conflicts. For example, ask "How do the Power Rangers solve their conflicts?" "Can you think of some way they could solve their conflicts without fighting?" Children can draw and write stories about this. They can also write alternative stories and stories from the points of view of different television characters on the same program.

Class Meetings. Hold class meetings to solve problems, using the win-win approach with the whole group. This is discussed more fully in the next chapter.

PART 3

Creating a Conflict Resolution Curriculum

CHAPTER 8

The Win-Win Classroom:
A Total Approach

A conflict resolution curriculum is more than teaching a particular set of concepts and skills to children. To be most effective and meaningful, conflict resolution needs to pervade all aspects of classroom life and become a total approach—a way of being together. This is especially true for young children, who learn best from direct experience[7].

A win-win classroom includes children in decision-making and problem solving about things they care about. Ask the children such questions as:

- What do you think would be a fair way to feed the new class fish so everyone gets a chance?
- We've been having a problem when we line up to go to lunch. What do you think we should do?
- Several people want to be Dorothy in *The Wizard of Oz* play this afternoon. Do you have ideas about how we can do this?

Implementing the Win-Win Approach

In the example that follows, a kindergarten teacher uses a win-win approach to solve a group problem. The way this teacher works with the group of children reflects the conflict resolution process described throughout this

---

7. For additional information about creating a classroom that supports a total approach to conflict resolution see *Ways We Want Our Class To Be* by the Developmental Studies Center (Oakland, CA: Developmental Studies Center, 1996) and *Teaching Young Children in Violent Times* by Diane E. Levin (Cambridge, MA: Educators for Social Responsibility, 1994).

book, which can be used to solve a range of problems and conflicts that arise in a classroom between individual children and between adults and children. Both the children and the teacher contribute ideas that eventually lead to a solution that all can agree to.

DISCUSSION	COMMENTARY
Teacher: I've noticed a problem that I think we need to talk about. There's been a lot of arguing and fighting in the block area lately. Have you noticed this? What do you think about it?	The teacher states *the problem* as one shared by all, without expressing blame or guilt.
Kim: Karimah said my building wasn't nice.	
Karimah: No, I didn't. I said it wasn't nice, then I said it was nice.	Children can respond and talk to each other, not just to the teacher.
Josh: Armando crashed blocks down on top of where I was making something.	
Armando: It was an accident. My tower fell down.	
Teacher: What do you think made the tower fall down?	She tries to help him focus on *logical causality.*
Armando: Somebody bumped into it.	

DISCUSSION	COMMENTARY
Teacher: So somebody bumped into Armando's tower, and then some blocks fell onto Josh's building? [Their heads nod.]	As the teacher uses *active listening*, she helps all the children connect to what is being discussed.
Armando: Then Josh started fighting.	
Teacher: So we do have a problem with fighting in the block area. It sounds like lots of different things are happening to cause the fights. Any ideas about what to do?	She *summarizes* the problem in terms the children can understand. Then she tries to get the children to *brainstorm possible solutions.*
Danielle: Too many kids in the blocks.	
Teacher: So you think too many children are playing in the block area? [Danielle and other children shake their heads in agreement.]	She uses *active listening* again.
Derrick: We should change the sign.	
Teacher: How would we do that?	She helps Derrick think about how his ideas would be put into practice. This makes his idea understandable to other children.
Derrick: Put a different number on it. Put four on it.	
Teacher: Okay, you think we could say four children instead of five can play in the block area? [Derrick nods in agreement.] Are there other ideas?	The teacher clarifies what his plan will mean in practice. The teacher is not passing judgment on the practicality or merit of the children's ideas. There are no right or wrong answers here.

DISCUSSION	COMMENTARY
Clarence: Just say, "You can't fight in the blocks. You have to go someplace else if you fight."	
Teacher: So we could tell people to go play in another area if they fight in the block area. Any other ideas?	The teacher continues to invite other ideas during this brainstorming period.
Teresa: Make a different block area. This one is too squishy.	
Teacher: How could we make a different block area?	Again, she tries to get the child to translate her idea into practice
Teresa: Make it bigger. Make a bigger rug.	
Teacher: Does anyone have an idea of how we could make the rug space in the block area bigger?	She gets all the children involved in thinking about how to make one possible solution work.
Leland: Move the green shelf. That'll make it bigger.	
Teacher: We could move the green shelf over. We could push it back farther onto the floor and that would make the rug area bigger. So, that's three ideas of what we can try. One is to say only four children can play in the blocks instead of five; one is to tell children who fight in blocks to go to another place to play; and the third is to move the shelf and make the block area bigger. Which idea shall we try first?	The children have come up with several ideas. The teacher summarizes without passing judgment. Then she helps them focus on choosing one to try.

DISCUSSION	COMMENTARY
Clarence: Make people go away from the blocks if they fight.	
Teacher: We could try that, but that might be kind of hard for me. I would have to keep telling people to leave the block area, and I might feel like a grumpy and mean teacher if I do that. Could we try one of the other ideas first? I think that would be better for me. [This seems to make sense to Clarence, and he nods yes.]	The teacher expresses how she feels about Clarence's solution with an "I" statement. She does not pass judgment on Clarence's idea. She gives all of the children an opportunity to see things from her point of view as the teacher and to respond to her needs.
Marie: Let's make the block area bigger. Let's move the shelf.	
Teacher: Do people want to try that? [Heads nod.] Does everyone agree? [All heads nod.] Well, I like this idea too. We all agree on that one.	They find a win-win solution—a solution that everyone, including the teacher, can agree to and like.
Teacher: Let's try moving the shelf and see how it works. Let's see if moving the shelf can help stop arguing and fighting in the block area. We'll talk about this in a few days and see how it's working. We can try another idea if we need to.	She assures the children they will have a chance to discuss how their solution works and revise it as needed.

Throughout this discussion, the teacher is the leader and helps ensure that the children reach a conclusion they all can agree to, including the teacher. |

Sharing Power

Giving children a say about what happens in the classroom and how it happens involves taking a look at the issue of power. This teacher is sharing her power with the children, but she is not giving up her power. She maintains her leadership role as teacher, guiding the problem-solving process along. When a solution is suggested that she does not feel is appropriate, she says why it is not a good solution for her in the form of an "I" statement: "I would have to keep telling people to leave the block area, and I might feel like a grumpy and mean teacher if I do that."

A win-win solution in a discussion like the one above occurs when the teacher helps children find a solution that everyone, including the teacher, can agree to and like. She uses her power to create a scaffolding that helps the children succeed at finding a positive solution that they would not have been able to come up with on their own.

We have found it helpful to think of the power relationship between adults and children as falling along a continuum. The following diagram represents this relationship. You can use it to take a reading of the overall balance of power in your classroom.

Key Elements to Problem Solving

The process this teacher uses to reach a win-win solution consists of the key elements in problem solving:

- Clarify the problem and see how it is shared by everyone.
- Talk about the problem.
- Brainstorm solutions.
- Consider the different solutions.
- Choose a solution to try.
- Reflect on how the solution works in practice.

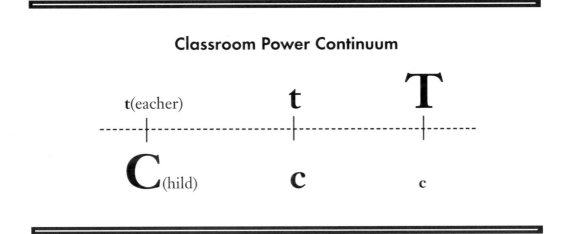

Classroom Power Continuum

In classrooms that fall at the far right of the continuum, teachers make most of the decisions, including how space is organized, classroom routines, what is studied, and when and how it is studied. A large capital T characterizes the teacher's power in this kind of classroom. Children, on the other hand, have little or no input on how things are done. A lowercase C characterizes their power.

On the far left of the continuum are teachers who leave many or most decisions about classroom life up to children—what they will do and when, how to arrange the room, what they want to learn. In this classroom, the teacher, represented by a lowercase T, gives up most of the power to children, represented by a capital C.

The win-win classroom is one in which teachers and children share power somewhere in the center of the continuum. Teachers help children use their power by participating in decision-making in ways that feel safe and are appropriate to children's developmental level and experience. As their participation and skills in resolving conflicts grow, children build their own inner resources for regulating themselves and acting fairly toward others. In a win-win classroom where everyone participates and feels part of the group, a strong sense of community usually develops.

Classroom decisions rarely remain at the same place along the continuum. Different kinds of situations lead to different levels of power sharing. You might find it helpful to use this continuum as a tool for looking at various situations with children in your class in terms of power and power sharing.

Conflict Resolution Throughout the Day

Children will need lots of practice and many opportunities to try out their developing peacemaking skills throughout the school day. The more you are able to help them do this, the more skillful they will become at peaceful conflict resolution. This means that conflict resolution needs to be embedded in daily classroom life and infused throughout the curriculum. You can begin to examine your classroom to see where conflict resolution skills such as perspective taking, active listening, and win-win solutions might be incorporated.

You can help children use conflict resolution skills in their own conflicts, whenever possible. When you see children having actual conflicts in the classroom, suggest they try using their conflict resolution skills at that moment: "Remember how Angela told Calvin how she felt? Can you do that right now with Jack?"

Here is one teacher's account of how she used *Best Day of the Week* to help children with a conflict[8]:

> *Adi seemed angry as the children came in from the playground. His face was scrunched up and he seemed too angry to speak. I suggested he draw how he was feeling. After Adi had been drawing for awhile, I asked him what had happened. His drawing showed three faces, his being the angry one with arms outstretched in a punch, with the letters "SRPD" (for stupid) and "MADY" (for mad). (See figure 10a.) Adi explained that he, Daniel, and Michael had been playing in the sandbox. Adi had wanted to build a tunnel under the sand structure they were all working on, but the others had not.*
>
> *As Adi was sharing his drawing with me, Michael and Daniel came over to the table. We talked a little bit about the different versions of what happened outside, and Adi explained his picture to them. I said I thought they could make a compromise with each other. I reminded them of Calvin and Angela in the story we had read, then went away for a bit.*
>
> *When I came back, they all yelled, "We worked it out!" They had drawn a picture of what their new sand structure would look like. (See figure 10b.) Their feelings of joy and pride in solving the problem were reflected in their drawing. The process of doing the drawing together had helped dissipate the bad feelings the three had shared earlier.*

---

8. Thanks to Meg Bruton of Fayerweather Street School in Cambridge, MA, for sharing this example.

Figure 10a
Adi's drawing of his conflict on the playground.

Figure 10b
The drawing Adi did with his friends showing how to work out their conflict.

Here are some other ideas to help you infuse conflict resolution skills throughout the curriculum and bring an awareness of conflict resolution to children throughout the day:

Conflict Corner. Try setting up a conflict corner where children can experiment with their developing conflict resolution skills. You can supply sock puppets, stick puppets, cardboard point of view feet, a "Stop—Think" sign, crayons and paper for drawing, feeling photos, and other props. Add books with stories that deal with conflicts that you can use with children and that children can use on their own. The books annotated in chapter 9 will help you get started.

Class Meetings. You can make conflict resolution an ongoing discussion topic at class meetings by using experiences that come up in the classroom.

Ask children at class meetings if they had any conflicts during the day, what they did to try to solve them, and what did and didn't work. Class meetings can also be a time to solve group problems and make decisions using the win-win approach. Be on the lookout for issues to bring to the group that are important to the children and about which you feel comfortable sharing your power and decision making.

Lists. As a class, build a repertoire of experience with conflict and conflict resolution. Make ongoing lists that record children's ideas, words, and successful strategies tried in conflicts. Keep these visible and refer to them regularly. Encourage children to try techniques that have worked for others and to invent new ones to add to the lists. Especially with younger children, try adding little pictures to each strategy to help them read and use them more easily.

Class Books. Children can make books with pictures or writing about conflicts they have had. Individual drawings and stories can be put into a large class book titled "Conflicts We Have Had," and it can be put in the conflict corner.

Tallies. Children can do surveys in which they tally information about conflicts. Survey questions might include the following:

- How many conflicts have you had this week?
- What do you do when you have a conflict? (Give several choices.)
- How many conflicts have we had as a class this week?
- How many ways can we think of to solve this conflict?

Graphs. Children can complete simple graphs to show their opinions about a conflict in a story. After reading Dr. Seuss' *Butter Battle Book*, for example, you can ask, "Do you think the Yooks and the Zooks could solve their conflict without fighting?" Have children count the number of yes and no votes, then fill in yes and no bars on a graph.

Infuse conflict resolution into all curriculum areas. Try helping children use conflict resolution skills when they are working together on projects in math, science, art, literacy, and other curriculum areas. Ask questions like,

"Can you practice active listening right now while Jenna is talking?" "Can you think of a win-win solution to planting these seeds so that everyone gets a chance?"

For additional ways to connect conflict resolution ideas to all areas of your classroom, see the curriculum webs in chapter 9.

Resources for Building a Conflict Resolution Curriculum

As we have worked with teachers on conflict resolution, we have found that the most effective approaches generally provide structure and meaningful starting points to help children organize their ideas and actions in concrete ways, but are flexible and open enough so that ideas can evolve and change. The following four resources (puppets, feeling photos, curriculum webs, and children's books) are a few examples of a range of effective approaches to conflict resolution we have observed in classrooms. They illustrate a range of possibilities for how to build a holistic conflict resolution curriculum with young children.

Puppets

As we have suggested throughout this guide, you can use puppets to work on many conflict resolution skills with young children[9]. Puppets provide a concrete and visible way to teach these vital skills and are a powerful supplement to using "words" to talk about conflict. Puppets can be especially helpful with children who have limited language ability as well as with children who have a hard time sitting through and participating in long conversations.

---

9. *This section on puppets is adapted from* Teaching Young Children in Violent Times: Building a Peaceable Classroom *by Diane E. Levin (Cambridge, MA: Educators for Social Responsibility, 1994). Thanks to William Kreidler for his contribution to our understanding of how to use puppets to work on conflict resolution with children.*

Using Puppets to Enhance a Conflict Resolution Curriculum

You can start with the cut-out puppets of Calvin and Angela provided at the end of this guide (or make your own cut-out figures). Tape the cut-out characters to rulers, chopsticks, or craft sticks. Use them to help you tell the story. Stop as you go along to:

- ask questions about the story.
- have children ask questions of Calvin and Angela and hear what they say.
- try out different solutions and scenarios with Angela and Calvin.

Gradually you can ask the children to take a greater role in using the puppets to tell the story.

Later, introduce puppets that are more generic than the Calvin and Angela puppets. Start with basic, small puppets that are less likely to suggest fighting or aggression (as puppets that cover the hand often do). For instance, make puppets by cutting small figures out of cardboard. Glue magazine photographs of diverse people to the cardboard figures and glue to wooden tongue depressors or craft sticks. Simple puppets made from old socks with buttons sewn on for eyes are also easy to use and appealing to children, however children need a lot of help from you in learning how to use puppets productively and nonviolently. Often the first thing a child does with a puppet—especially if it fits over the hand—is to punch someone else. Start with simple play and use the puppets yourself at first, concretely modeling the kinds of things children can do with them.

As they work with the puppets, try to help the children tap into the wide range of skills they are learning from working on conflict resolution in the classroom, like using the words they have learned, brainstorming solutions to problems, and practicing communication skills.

How Puppets Promote Goals of Conflict Resolution Curriculum

Puppets provide young children with a safe and meaningful way to live and work together in a peaceable classroom. They help children:

- actively work on the specific skills discussed in this book.
- experience a sense of control and mastery through reenacting conflicts from their own experience and determining what happens.
- develop confidence and skill as they try out new ideas, take risks, and practice new skills.

How Puppets Match Children's Developmental Level

Used appropriately, puppets also provide an effective way to help young children work on the vital cognitive skills used in resolving conflicts. As children work with puppets, they can be helped to:

- move from static thinking about experiences to more dynamic thinking because they actually can use the puppets to transform and vary events over and over.

- move from seeing one aspect of a situation at a time to seeing many aspects and from seeing isolated parts of a situation to a more integrated whole as they use puppets to organize events into a logical sequence and make logical causal connections between them.

- shift from seeing only one point of view (usually their own) to seeing more than one viewpoint and even how the two views interact with one another as the puppets act out their various roles and perspectives in a less threatening situation.

Feeling Photos

As we have discussed throughout this book, learning about the feelings that are part of conflict and its resolution is a vital part of the process for children. Yet, because of how they tend to think, young children tend to have difficulty recognizing the feelings of another when those feelings are different from their own, identifying feelings that cannot be identified by facial expressions and other external indicators, and understanding the logical causality of feelings. Feeling photos are a fruitful starting point for talking about feelings in ways that take young children's thinking into account[10].

Feeling photos are photographs of people with facial expressions that capture a wide range of human emotions. You can cut them out of magazines and gradually build a collection. Or you can purchase commercially prepared materials like those listed below. Be sure to include images that represent a

---

10. Thanks to the Early Childhood Peaceable Classroom Group at Educators for Social Responsibility who worked with Diane Levin to develop this idea.

diversity of people. If possible, laminate the photos so children can easily handle them. You can also purchase special posters and books with photographs of people showing emotions.

Figure 11
The feeling photos pictured here are from the "Emotions Poster," available from Childswork/Childsplay.

Using Feeling Photos to Build a Conflict Resolution Curriculum

Here are ways to use feeling photos with children:

- Hang the feeling photos on a free-standing display board so they can be used flexibly and in many parts of the day.
- Encourage children to select feeling photos that show how they feel and bring them to a class meeting. Ask children to show the photo they chose and tell how they are feeling. Some children might also tell what they need, especially if they are feeling bad.
- Have children pick photos to show how they feel during a conflict, and talk about these feelings.
- Make up stories, draw, or write stories that go with the photos.
- Sequence several photos and make up a story to go with them.
- Classify photos into groups of feelings.

You could also put the photos in the conflict corner for children to use in their own ways.

Resources for Feeling Photos

The following resources are available from Childswork/Childsplay, c/o Genesis Direct, Inc., 100 Plaza Drive, Secaucus, NJ 07094-3613 (1-800-962-1141):

Face Your Feelings: A Book to Help Children Learn about Feelings, developed by L.E. Shapiro, 1993.
Fifty-two pictures of racially diverse children and adults of all ages expressing feelings. The accompanying text with each picture explains what caused the feeling that is being expressed.

Face It! Card Deck
Fifty-two faces of kids, teens, and adults with diverse facial expressions on a deck of playing cards.

Emotions Poster
Twenty-eight photographs of racially diverse young children expressing a wide range of feelings.

"Everyone Has Feelings" Poster.
A large poster (24 by 37 inches) with thirty-six photos of diverse people of all ages expressing a wide range of expressions.

Curriculum Webs

Curriculum webs provide a valuable resource for bringing order to your efforts to develop a curriculum that can work for you and the children[11]. Webs can help you:

- keep track of and organize a great deal of information about your conflict resolution curriculum.
- see connections between various aspects of your conflict resolution curriculum.
- work out how conflict resolution activities connect to various traditional subject areas.
- brainstorm possible new activities to add to what you have already done.
- communicate effectively and efficiently with parents and other school personnel about the conflict resolution activities in your classroom.

---

11. For a more detailed account of curriculum webs, see "Weaving Curriculum Webs: Planning, Guiding, and Recording Curriculum Activities in the Day Care Classroom" by D. Levin in Day Care and Early Education (Summer, 1986).

Curriculum Web I: Curricular Themes That Can Be Developed Using *Best Day of the Week*

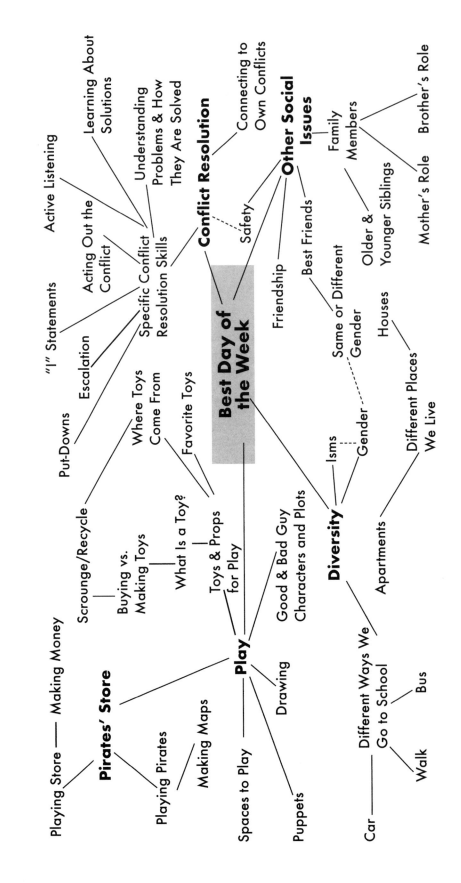

Curriculum Web II: Subject Areas That Can Be Integrated into *Best Day of the Week* Activities

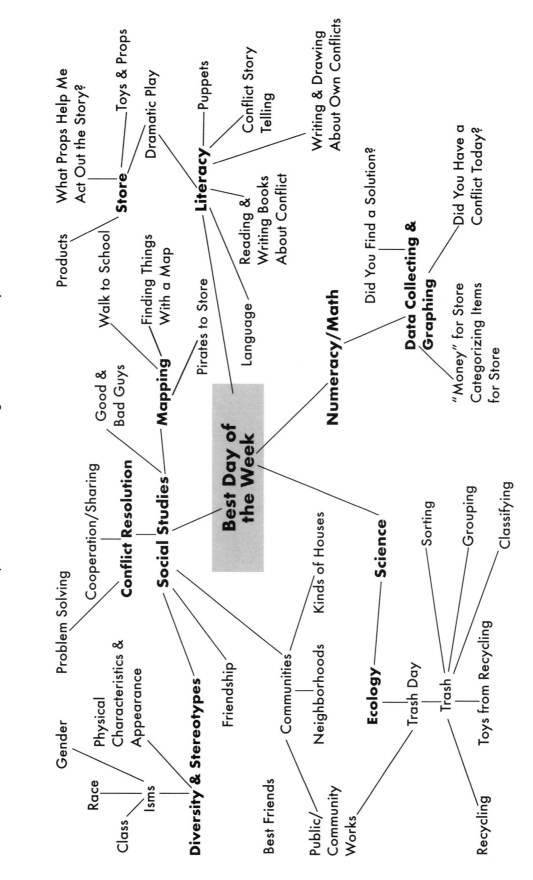

Using Other Children's Books

Besides *Best Day of the Week*, there are many wonderful children's books that can help you build your conflict resolution curriculum. Listed below are several of the books that we have found to be particularly well-suited to the task[12]. Reading a variety of the recommended children's books before working on conflict resolution with the children will help you determine how you want to present a given book to the children and what questions about the book you will ask the children to start discussion. It will also allow you to decide how you can use the books to work on specific conflict resolution skills. As we have indicated in the annotations, some books are especially well-suited for working on particular skills.

For instance, you might decide to use *Swimmy* by Leo Lionni. It is a story about a school of small fish who work together to help Swimmy solve his conflict with a big fish. After reading the story to the children, you could ask such questions as the following:

- What do you think Swimmy said to the other little fish to get them to help?
- What could Swimmy have said to the big fish to try to work the problem out?
- Tell us about a time you got someone to help you solve a problem. How did you get that person to help you?

Figure 12
Swimmy is a good book to use for working on conflict resolution skills with children.

---

12. *Special thanks to Christine Gerzon for her assistance in finding and annotating many of the conflict resolution books listed here.*

Recommended Children's Books

Bruchac, Joseph. *The First Strawberries: A Cherokee Story.* New York: Dial, 1993.
A traditional tale about how the wonder of strawberries helps a wife and husband settle their conflict. Useful for discussing adult conflicts.

Bourgeois, Paulette. *Franklin Is Bossy.* New York: Scholastic, 1993.
Franklin learns about the give-and-take inherent in friendship. Useful for discussing the importance of talking about feelings.

Clifton, Lucille. *Three Wishes.* New York: Viking, 1976.
A magic penny leads to a conflict and solution between best friends, Lena and Victor. Useful for discussing lose-lose solutions, how conflicts escalate, and conflicts with friends.

dePaola, Tomie. *The Knight and the Dragon.* New York: Putnam, 1990.
The knight and the dragon prepare to fight until the librarian of the kingdom comes up with a better idea. Good for talking about finding peaceful solutions.

Graham, Bob. *This Is Our House.* Cambridge, MA: Candlewick, 1996.
George says only he can use the large cardboard carton house and refuses to let other children play in it. But they have other ideas. Good for working on prejudices and anti-bias, conflicts over playmates, and sharing play materials.

Greenfield, Eloise. *First Pink Light.* New York: Black Butterfly, 1976.
Mother and son negotiate a conflict in this poignant story about waiting for the father to come home.

Guback, Georgia. *Luka's Quilt.* New York: Greenwillow, 1994.
Luka and her grandmother have a conflict over how the traditional quilt her grandmother is making for her should look. They come up with a solution that satisfies them both. Excellent for discussing win-win solutions.

Havill, Juanita. *Jamaica and Brianna.* Boston: Houghton Mifflin, 1993.
Two friends make hurtful comments about each other's boots until they realize that what they say hurts. Good for discussions about different points of view and put-downs, as well as conflicts over what to buy and how to look.

———. *Jamaica Tag-Along*. Boston: Houghton Mifflin, 1989.
Jamaica is distressed that her older brother won't let her play. Another child messes up her sand castle. In the end, all three children find a way to work together. Excellent for discussing different points of view, how one's actions affect others, and conflicts among siblings.

Hoffman, Mary. *Amazing Grace*. New York: Dial, 1991.
Grace wants to play the role of Peter Pan in the school play. Another child tells her she can't be Peter Pan because she is Black. But she can play the role, and she does! A good book to talk about problem solving and counteracting bias statements.

Jones, Rebecca C. *Matthew and Tilly*. New York: Dutton, 1991.
Matthew and Tilly are best friends until Matthew breaks Tilly's purple crayon. A good story for working on conflicts between friends, escalation, and different kinds of solutions to conflict.

Lionni, Leo. *Six Crows*. New York: Scholastic, 1988.
The farmer and the crows fight over the same wheat field until they learn the value of communication. Good for focusing on communicating feelings and needs.

———. *Swimmy*. New York: Scholastic, 1963.
A small fish organizes the other fish to stand up to the big fish. Can be used to talk about many aspects of conflict resolution.

Piers, Helen. *Long Neck and Thunderfoot*. London: Puffin, 1982.
Two dinosaurs, who are afraid of each other because they look different, learn how to make beautiful music together. Especially helpful for working on perspective taking and anti-bias issues.

Popov, Nikolai. *Why?* New York: North South, 1996.
A picture book without words about the violent escalation of a conflict between frogs and mice, which ends in devastation. (Not recommended for very young children.) Good for helping older children explore lose-lose solutions to conflict and escalation.

Scieszka, Jon. *The True Story of the Three Little Pigs by A. Wolf*. New York: Scholastic, 1989.
The popular fairy tale told from the point of view of the Big Bad Wolf. Excellent for working on perspective taking.

Seuss, Dr. *The Butter Battle Book*. New York: Random House, 1984.
Engaged in a long-running battle, the Yooks and the Zooks develop more and more sophisticated weaponry as they attempt to outdo each other. Good for talking about escalation of conflict.

—————. *The Sneeches and Other Stories*. New York: Random House, 1961.
Three good stories about conflict. *The Sneeches* is especially good for talking about anti-bias issues. *The Zax* is good for talking about lose-lose solutions to conflicts.

Silverman, Erica. *Don't Fidget a Feather*. New York: Macmillan, 1994.
Duck and Gander always compete over who's best. One day their game over who can stand still longer leads to big trouble, until one of them decides not to compete. Excellent for discussing win-lose, lose-lose, and win-win solutions, as well as competitive (winner-loser) games.

Wildsmith, Brian. *The Owl and the Woodpecker*. New York: Oxford University Press, 1971.
Owl cannot sleep since Woodpecker moved into the tree next to him. Woodpecker will not move...until a big storm. A good story for teaching about points of view and perspective taking.

Zolotow, Charlotte. *The Hating Book*. New York: Harper Trophy, 1969.
A little girl learns the value of communication and preserves her friendship with her best friend. Good for focusing on relationships and communication skills.

Resources

Carlsson-Paige, Nancy, and Diane E. Levin. "'The Butter Battle Book': Uses and Abuses with Young Children." *Young Children* 41 (March 1986): 37-42.

———. "Making Peace in Violent Times." *Young Children* 48 (November 1992): 4-13.

———. *The War Play Dilemma: Balancing Needs and Values in the Early Childhood Classroom.* New York: Teachers College, 1987.

———. *Who's Calling the Shots? How to Respond Effectively to Children's Fascination with War Play, War Toys, and Violent TV.* Gabriola Island, BC, Can.: New Society, 1990.

Collins, Mark, and Joan Dalton. *Becoming Responsible Learners: Strategies for Positive Classroom Management.* Portsmouth, NY: Heinemann, 1990.

Dalton, Joan, and Marilyn Watson. *Among Friends: Classrooms Where Caring and Learning Prevail.* Oakland, CA: Developmental Studies Center, 1997.

Developmental Studies Center. *Blueprints for a Collaborative Classroom: Twenty-five Designs for Partner and Group Work.* Oakland, CA: Developmental Studies Center, 1997.

———. *Ways We Want Our Class to Be: Class Meetings that Build Commitment to Kindness and Learning.* Oakland, CA: Developmental Studies Center, 1996.

DeVries, Rita, and Betty Zan. *Moral Classrooms, Moral Children: Creating a Constructivist Atmosphere in Early Education.* New York: Teachers College, 1994.

Edwards, Carolyn P. *Promoting Social and Moral Development in Young Children: Creative Approaches for the Classroom.* New York: Teachers College, 1986.

Family, Friends, and Community. "Voices of Love and Freedom: A K-12 Multicultural Literature, Ethics, and Prevention Program." *K-5 Elementary Catalogue*. Boston, MA: Judge Baker Children's Center, 1995-96.

Garbarino, James. *Raising Children in a Socially Toxic Environment*. San Francisco: Jossey-Bass, 1995.

Hopkins, Susan, and Jeffry Winters. *Discover the World: Empowering Children to Value Themselves, Others, and the Earth*. Gabriola Island, BC, Can.: New Society, 1990.

Kreidler, William J. *Creative Conflict Resolution: More than 200 Activities for Keeping Peace in the Classroom*. Glencoe, IL: Scott Foresman, 1984.

———. *Elementary Perspectives: Teaching Concepts of Peace and Conflict*. Cambridge, MA: Educators for Social Responsibility, 1990.

———. *Teaching Conflict Resolution through Children's Literature*. New York: Scholastic Professional Books, 1994.

Kohn, Alfie. *Beyond Discipline: From Compliance to Community*. Alexandria, VA: Association for Supervision and Curriculum Development, 1996.

———. *Punished by Rewards: The Trouble with Gold Stars, Incentive Plans, A's, Praise, and Other Bribes*. Boston: Houghton Mifflin, 1993.

Lantieri, Linda, and Janet Patti. *Waging Peace in Our Schools*. Boston: Beacon Press, 1996.

Levin, Diane E., *Remote Control Childhood? Combating the Hazards of Media Culture*. Washington, DC: National Association for the Education of Young Children, 1998.

———.*Teaching Young Children in Violent Times: Building a Peaceable Classroom*. Cambridge, MA: Educators for Social Responsibility, 1994.

———. "Weaving Curriculum Webs: Planning, Guiding, and Recording Curriculum Activities in the Day Care Classroom." *Day Care and Early Education* 15 (Summer 1986), 16-19.

Levin, Diane E., and Nancy Carlsson-Paige. "The Mighty Morphin Power Rangers: Teachers Voice Concern." *Young Children* 50 (September 1995), 67-72.

Mastellone, Flavia Rose. *Finding Peace Through Conflict: Teaching Skills for Resolving Conflicts and Building Peace.* Amherst, MA: National Association for Mediation in Education, 1993.

Miller, Sarah, Janine Brodine, and Terri Miller, eds. *Safe by Design: Planning for Peaceful School Communities.* Seattle, WA: Committee for Children, 1996.

Ramsey, Patricia G. *Making Friends in School: Promoting Peer Relationships in Early Childhood.* New York: Teachers College, 1991.

Trawick-Smith, Jeffrey. *Interactions in the Classroom: Facilitating Play in the Early Years.* New York: Merrill, 1994.

Wichert, S. *Keeping the Peace: Practicing Cooperation and Conflict Resolution with Preschoolers.* Gabriola Island, BC, Can.: New Society, 1989.

Puppet Cut-Outs

Make simple stick puppets of Angela and Calvin to model conflict resolution skills. Tape the cut-out characters to rulers, chopsticks, or craft sticks and use them to help you tell the story. For durability, you may want to glue them to cardboard or laminate them.

Other Redleaf Publications

All the Colors We Are: The Story of How We Get Our Skin Color - Outstanding full-color photographs showcase the beautiful diversity of human skin color and offers children a simple, accurate explanation of how we are the color we are. Bilingual English/Spanish.

Big As Life, Volumes 1 and 2- The first comprehensive curriculum to weave multicultural and anti-bias activities naturally throughout the program. Stacey York, author of the best-selling *Roots and Wings,* provides a guide to planning inclusive curriculum and over 1500 activities in two volumes.

For the Love of Children: Daily Affirmations for People Who Care for Children - An empowering book filled with quotes, stories, and affirmations for each day of the year.

Making It Better: Activities for Children Living in a Stressful World - This important book offers bold new information about the physical and emotional effects of stress, trauma, and violence on children today and gives teachers and caregivers the confidence to help children survive, thrive, and learn.

Reflecting Children's Lives - A practical guide to help you put children and childhood at the center of your curriculum. Rethink and refresh your ideas about scheduling, observations, play, materials, space, and emergent themes.

Those Icky Sticky Smelly Cavity-Causing but...Invisible Germs - This is an imaginative tool to help children develop good toothbrushing habits. Bilingual English/Spanish.

Those Itsy-Bitsy Teeny-Tiny Not-So-Nice Head Lice - Teaches children and adults about how head lice are spread, commonly used methods for getting rid of lice, and ways to prevent the spread and reinfestation of head lice. Bilingual English/Spanish

Those Mean Nasty Dirty Downright Disgusting but...Invisible Germs - This popular children's book shows the five germ characters that cause illness. Teach children the importance of hand washing. Bilingual English/Spanish.

1-800-423-8309